BELVEDERE

by

by George Crenshaw

TOR

A TOM DOHERTY ASSOCIATES BOOK

This is a work of fiction. All the characters and events portrayed in this book are fictional, and any resemblance to real people or incidents is purely coincidental.

BELVEDERE

A TOR Book

Published by Tom Doherty Associates, 8-10 W. 36th St., New York, City, NY 10018

First printing, April 1984

ISBN: 812-56-220-8
Can. Ed. 812-56-221-6

Printed in the United States of America

"OH, RELAX, ALL THAT ABOMINABLE SNOWMAN JAZZ IS JUST A WILD FIGMENT OF IMAGINATION."

"I'VE ADDED A JACUZZI AND WET BAR TO YOUR DOGHOUSE, BUT THE ZONING COMMISSION WON'T ALLOW A BONE CELLAR."

"... AND HE WAS WHITE WITH BLACK SPOTS AND LAST SEEN WITH A HUGE MOUTHFULL OF SALAMI ! "

" NOW YOU'VE DONE IT ! "

" THE NEXT TIME YOU TWO CELEBRATE MY BIRTHDAY, HOW ABOUT TAKING ME ALONG? "

" ADMIT IT. YOU'RE MAD ABOUT SOMETHING, AREN'T YOU? "

"EVER THINK OF GIVING YOUR BRAIN TO SCIENCE? OR WOULD THEY ACCEPT A GIFT THAT SMALL?"

"WE'RE PLAYING COPS AND ROBBERS."

" NOT BAD. NOT BAD. HE SHAVED TWO SECONDS OFF HIS BEST TIME. "

"HEY, OLD BUDDY - THIS IS NO TIME FOR FUN AND GAMES!"

"SURE, IT'S ELIMINATED TABLE BEGGING, BUT I STILL SAY THIS IS RIDICULOUS!"

"NOW THERE'S A DOGGIE TRICK YOU SELDOM SEE."

" LOOK AT IT THIS WAY – ON THE MOON YOU WOULD ONLY WEIGH 35 POUNDS. "

"GOOD HEAVENS, LET HIM PRACTICE HIS BOWLING IF HE WANTS. WHAT CAN HE HURT?"

"IF YOU'RE LOOKING FOR VIOLENCE AND EXCITEMENT, HOW ABOUT BATHING BELVEDERE?"

" LOOK, DO WE COMPLAIN WHEN YOU HOWL TOO LOUD AT THE MOON ? "

"LOOK, HE BAGGED ONE! DON'T QUESTION **WHAT** OR **HOW**!"

"OKAY, OKAY - CONGRATULATIONS, BELVEDERE. WE JUST VOTED YOU INTO OUR CLUB."

"GIVE IT UP. IT'LL NEVER WORK!"

" YOU REALIZE, OF COURSE, THAT AS A BIRD-WATCHER YOU ARE ALL WASHED UP ! "

"NOW THERE'S A DOGGIE TRICK YOU SELDOM SEE."

" THE HEART, STUPID!... YOU'RE SUPPOSED TO GO FOR THE HEART!"

" YES, DR. BARKUM IS EXPECTING YOUR DOG. "

"YOU CAN ALWAYS TELL AN OLD RETIRED SEA DOG."

"HERE WE ARE - 276 FEET BELOW SEA LEVEL. WHO WOULD EVER BELIEVE IT?!"

"WE ALWAYS KNOW WHEN HE WANTS SOMETHING."

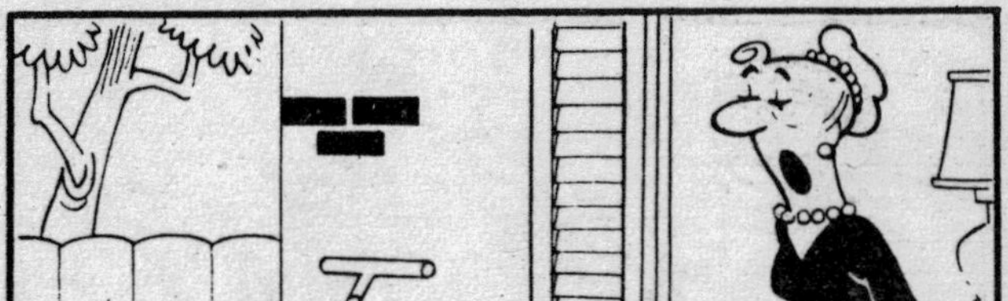

"I THOUGHT ORVILLE WAS SUPPOSED TO BE HELPING YOU ROLL THE SOD."

" I'M NOT THAT BAD A DRIVER, AND YOU KNOW IT. "

" CUTE DOG!...HOW SWEET OF HIM TO GIVE YOU SUCH A NICE BIG FRIENDLY HUG. "

" ADMIT IT. YOU'VE BEEN DRINKING AGAIN! "

"WE'RE 300 FEET BELOW SEA LEVEL, OLD BUDDY. IT'S HARD TO BELIEVE THIS WAS ONCE A HUGE INLAND OCEAN."

" SO YOUR RANGE BROKE DOWN — I KNEW HE'D THINK OF SOMETHING. "

" NOW WHAT HAPPENED TO MY OUTBOARD MOTOR? "

"NO, I WILL NOT FOIL-WRAP YOUR BONES BEFORE YOU BURY THEM."

"MAYDAY! MAYDAY! RED ALERT!"

" AREN'T THOSE MY GOLF CLUBS ? "

"HARKEN ! DO I HEAR THE CRUMPLE OF PAPER HERALDING THE UNFOLDMENT OF A FRESH BOX OF CRACKERS ? "

" OH, JUST BE QUIET AND DRIVE. I'M TRYING TO SNOOZE. "

" DID YOU TAKE THE FRESH FLOWERS IN TO ORVILLE ? "

" YOU'LL LIKE HIS BATHTUB GIN. "

" BELVEDERE AND JEZEBEL AND CHI-CHI HAVE TAKEN OVER THE HOUSE UNTIL WE ACCEDE TO THEIR DEMANDS. "

"WHAT DO YOU MEAN, SORRY, YOU'VE RENTED OUT YOUR DOGHOUSE?"

" IT'S FROM THE DOG BELVEDERE NEXT DOOR—IT SAYS,
'SORRY I BUSTED YOUR CAR WINDOW.' "

"I DON'T THINK HE'S LOST AT ALL. HE'S JUST CASHING IN ON OUR KEEP-EM-HAPPY-'TIL-THE-OWNER-SHOWS-UP POLICY."

"AFTER YOU FINISH YOUR BREW, LET'S GO FOR A RIDE."

"IF YOU WANTED AN **AIR CONDITIONER**, WHY DIDN'T YOU SAY SO ?"

" NEVER MIND THE PEACE SIGN.... RUN ! "

" WHY CAN'T HE JUST BARK AT PEDDLERS LIKE OTHER DOGS DO?"

"SHE WAS PERFECTLY HAPPY WITH THIS OLD PERCH. THEN ONE DAY SHE WAS WATCHING THE GONG SHOW..."

" LET ME GUESS. . . IS IT TURTLE SOUP ? "

" I THOUGHT I HAD HIM IN A TOUGH SPOT THERE FOR A MINUTE. "

" BELVEDERE? I'M SORRY, HE'S BUSY DESTROYING THE UNIVERSE RIGHT NOW. CAN I TAKE A MESSAGE? "

" YOUR ELECTRIC BILL JUST CAME. "

" YOU HAVE INVENTED A CURE FOR ORVILLE'S SLEEP-WALKING? HOW? "

" THAT WAS **SOME** HOUSE PARTY YOU HAD LAST NIGHT. "

" BELVEDERE BROUGHT YOU A NICE SANDWICH, ORVY. AREN'T YOU GOING TO THANK HIM ? "

"THEY'RE NOT BURNED THAT BAD AND YOU KNOW IT!"

"A THOUSAND GARBAGE CANS IN THE COUNTY AND YOU HAD TO RAID THE BACK ALLEY OF AJAX-BLACKTOP!"

" BY GEORGE!... HE'S SPOTTED A BALD EAGLE."

"HE CERTAINLY MAKES THE JOB LOOK EASY!"

" HE GETS LAZIER EVERY DAY. "

"DO YOU HAVE TO KEEP PLAYING YOUR 'DEM BONES' TAPE?"

"SEE, CLANCY. I TOLD YOU HE'S NOT SUCH A BAD POOCH."

" THE NEXT TIME YOU TRAMP ACROSS A FRESH SIDEWALK, MAKE SURE IT ISN'T QUICK-DRYING! "

" ARE YOU GOING TO EAT IT OR CLIMB IT? "

"SO HE DOESN'T LIKE MY LEFTOVERS. DOES HE HAVE TO CALL THE FOOD AND DRUG ADMINISTRATION?"

"WELL, SO MUCH FOR PIRANHA FISHING."

"HE'S GOING TO WEAR OUT THAT BOOK OF FOSSIL SKELETONS."

"WHAT DO YOU MEAN, MY OLD GIRDLE FITS PERFECTLY? NOW TAKE THAT OFF!"

"I'M SORRY. WE DON'T HAVE ANY CHOCOLATE-COVERED BONES."

"IT ALL STARTED WHEN WE PUT A POCKET WATCH UNDER HIS BLANKET AS A PUPPY."

" NO WONDER YOU CAN'T GET THE LASSIE SHOW. YOU'RE WATCHING THE MICROWAVE OVEN. "

" HARD TO BELIEVE HE WAS ONCE THAT SPIRITED LITTLE QUARTERBACK AT OLD STATE U."

"WHY CAN'T HE JUST ROMP THROUGH THE PARK LIKE OTHER DOGS DO?"

"HEY! THAT WAS MY LUNCH!"

" ORVILLE FINALLY GOT BELVEDERE TO HEEL. HE RUBBED BARBECUE SAUCE ON HIS SOCKS. "

" HOW DO YOU WANT IT, FLUFF DRY OR STARCHED ? "

"FEEL PROUD. NOT MANY PEOPLE GET A SPEED TICKET DRIVING THROUGH A HOTEL LOBBY."

"HE SAYS HE'S WORKING HIS WAY THROUGH OBEDIENCE SCHOOL."

" GO RUN THE ELECTRIC CAN OPENER SO HE'LL GET OFF MY CHAIR. "

"ALL RIGHT, WHO WROTE **HELP** ON THE BOTTOM OF MY SKIS?"

"WHO NEEDS A MOOSE HORN—THE WAY YOU TWO WERE SNORING LAST NIGHT."

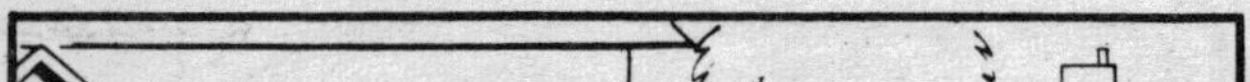

"LOOK. WOULDN'T IT BE EASIER TO JUST BARK AT PEDDLERS?"

"SO I SNEAKED SOME OATMEAL INTO HIS HAMBURGER AND HE'S PEEVED WITH ME. SO WHAT CAN A DOG DO?"

"WELL, HERE'S MUD IN YOUR EYE!"

" HE'S FINALLY FOUND SOMEONE TO LAUGH AT HIS CORNY JOKES."

" SEE? THIS IS WHAT YOU'RE SUPPOSED TO DO ! "

" CURIOUS HE'S SUDDENLY TAKEN SUCH A KEEN INTEREST IN KITE FLYING . "

" YA GOT ME, SID...I THOUGHT HE WAS **YOUR** DOG! "

"WOULD YOU MIND WHISTLING SOME OTHER TUNE?"

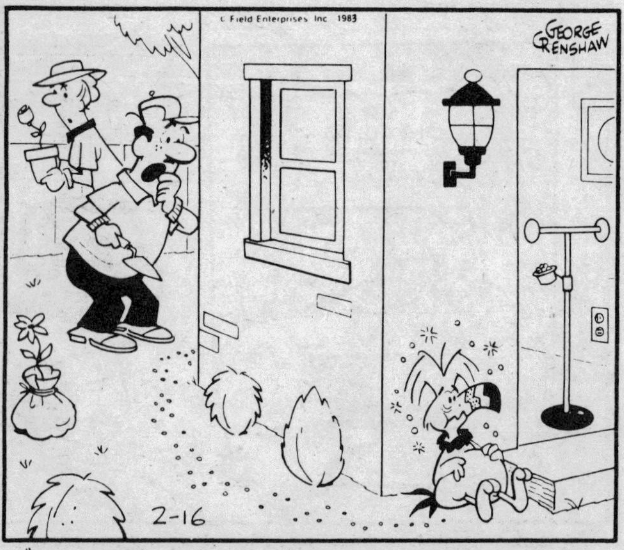

"NOW THAT'S STRANGE. I COULD HAVE SWORN MY SACK OF SEEDS WAS RIGHT HERE NEXT TO THE HOUSE."

" HE'S AROUND HERE SOMEWHERE. I KNOW IT! ..."

" LOOK, OLD BUDDY, I APPRECIATE THE NEW PUSH BROOM FOR MY BIRTHDAY, BUT WITH **TRAINING WHEELS**?"

"I THOUGHT YOU MIGHT BE LOOKING FOR THIS. THE GARAGE DOOR HAS BEEN GOING UP AND DOWN FOR THE PAST 10 MINUTES."

"AREN'T YOU DRESSED YET? THE FROTHINGHAMS AND THEIR DOG BELVEDERE WILL BE HERE IN FIVE MINUTES."

" IT'S THE ONLY WAY I CAN GET HIM TO EAT THE OFF-BRAND DOG FOOD. "

" OH, WELL, I DIDN'T FEEL MUCH LIKE PLAYING TODAY ANYWAY. "

"WELL, ARE YOU GOING TO APOLOGIZE FOR SPILLING THE GARBAGE OR SHALL I JUST PLAY YOUR ALIBI TAPE ?"

"I KNOW YOU'RE MAD AT ME, BUT IS THAT ANY WAY TO HANG MY PICTURE?"

" I THINK OUR NEW SIGN IS WORKING WITH THE NEIGHBOR'S DOG. "

" DON'T WORRY WHEN YOU COME BACK TO WORK, SCHMERTZ - THEY'RE GIVING BELVEDERE'S ROUTE TO ANOTHER CARRIER."

" HERE'S YOUR TROUBLE. "

" WHY DID WE EVER LET HIM WATCH 'LOVE BOAT'? "

"WHAT HAPPENED TO BELVEDERE?"

"JUST WHOSE IDEA WAS IT TO GIVE HIM A SAILBOAT AND A RUBBER DUCKIE FOR CHRISTMAS?"

"WHEN YOU TOLD HIM HE HAD TO SLEEP IN HIS DOGHOUSE, YOU SHOULD HAVE STIPULATED **OUTSIDE**!"

"DON'T WORRY ABOUT HIM. THEY DO WONDERS WITH HAIR TRANSPLANTS THESE DAYS."

"BREAK OUT THE BREADED FISH STICKS!"

" HELLO? GUINNESS BOOK OF WORLD RECORDS?..."

" STOP COMPLAINING! WE GOT YOU A PASSENGER SEAT, DIDN'T WE?"

"HE'LL DO ANYTHING TO BE DIFFERENT."

"JUST ONCE I WISH WE COULD GET AWAY FOR A FEW DAYS WITHOUT A SCENE."

"HE JUST FOUND OUT THE BUTCHER SHOP ACROSS THE STREET MOVED."

"YOU WEREN'T KIDDING! HE *IS* TRICKY!"

" PITY WE HAD TO GET UP SO EARLY AND LEAVE BELVEDERE BEHIND."

" FOR THE LIFE OF ME, I CAN'T FIND OUR NEW BOTTLE OF CHAMPAGNE."

"MAYBE WE SHOULDN'T HAVE GIVEN HER THE CRUMBS FROM THE RUM CAKE."

"AN ANONYMOUS NEIGHBOR HAS PRESENTED BELVEDERE WITH A FREE TRAINING COURSE IN RUSSIAN ROULETTE."

"NONE OF THE NEIGHBORS COULD GUESS YOUR WEIGHT AND AGE, SO I HAD TO TELL THEM."

" HE INVITED US TO HIS VICTORY PARTY? BUT HE HASN'T EVEN WON YET. "

" HE HAD TO HAVE A BUCKET SEAT."

" I DIDN'T SAY YOU WERE A BAD COOK, BUT LEMON MERINGUE HASH ! "

" WHY DO YOU EVER ASK HIM TO FIX ANYTHING ? "

"YOU DON'T SEE MANY DOG HOUSES WITH A CHANDELIER."

"WELL, ANSWER THE DOOR. MAYBE THE NEIGHBORS WANT TO GIVE ME A HUNDRED THOUSAND DOLLARS IF I SHIP YOU TO SIBERIA."

"BELVEDERE MADE THE COFFEE THIS MORNING. I HOPE IT'S NOT TOO STRONG."

"DON'T TELL BELVEDERE WE'RE GOING TO HAVE S-T-E-A..."

"HE'S SURRENDERING AGAIN. WHAT DO YOU SUPPOSE HE DID WRONG THIS TIME?"

"DON'T GIVE UP NOW - YOU'VE GOT A NO-HITTER GOING!"

" HE'S GETTING PRETTY GOOD. MAYBE WE SHOULD BUY HIM A REAL HARP. "

"MR. BOSWELL MUST HAVE PAINTED HIS PICKET FENCE."

"YOU'VE GOT A REAL PICTURE-BOOK SWING, ORVY. TOO BAD A FEW PAGES ARE MISSING."

"I THOUGHT YOU LOCKED HIM IN!"

"THEN THE POOCH SAYS, 'IT WORKS JUST LIKE A WATER PISTOL, DON'T IT?' AND BEFORE I COULD GET IT AWAY FROM HIM.."

" A GREAT PLACE TO BURY BONES...IS THAT ALL YOU HAVE TO SAY ? "

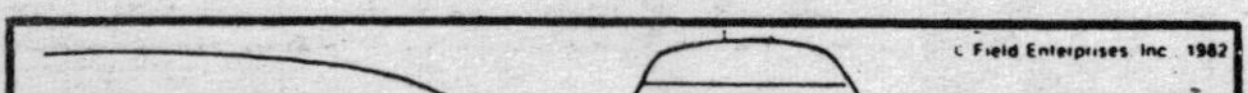

" HOW'D IT GO WITH YOUR BIG NEW KITE, FELLAS ? "

"WHAT A TIME-SAVER! WITH HER NEW MICROWAVE OVEN SHE CAN RUIN A MEAL THREE TIMES AS FAST."

"WHERE HAVE YOU BEEN?"

"WE'VE GOT TO GIVE HIM A KEY."

"BE PROUD. NOT MANY PEOPLE GO ON A WATER DIET AND GAIN FIVE GALLONS."

"YOU CAN ALWAYS TELL WHEN HE WANTS STEAK FOR DINNER."

"WE MIGHT AS WELL FORGET THE ELEMENT OF SURPRISE. BELVEDERE'S GOT EVERY POOCH IN TOWN RIGGED WITH A BEEPER."

"I'M AFRAID YOU CAN'T DECLARE WHAT YOUR DOG STEALS FROM YOUR REFRIGERATOR AS A CASUALTY LOSS."

"YESSIR! THERE'S A POOCH WITH A SENSE OF HUMOR!"

"YOU'RE NOT TAKING BELVEDERE TO CADDIE. YOU KNOW WE DON'T ALLOW HIM TO WATCH VIOLENCE."

"HE LIKES HIS COFFEE REAL STRONG."

" I WONDERED WHY HE'D BEEN BORROWING ICE CUBES ALL OVER THE NEIGHBORHOOD. "

" AND QUIT CALLING ME 'WARDEN'! "

"MAYBE WE SHOULD START CLOSING CHI CHI'S WINDOW. I'M NOT TOO CRAZY ABOUT HER NEW FRIENDS!"

" SAFE ! "

" YOU MUST BE MISTAKEN, DOCTOR. NO ONE AT THIS NUMBER CALLED ABOUT A NOSE JOB. "

" SO THAT'S WHY THE STAIRS ARE GREASED. "

" DO YOU ALWAYS HAVE TO BRING YOUR BLOODHOUND FRIENDS ALONG WHEN YOU CADDIE ? "

" THAT'S RIGHT. A LARGE PIZZA SMOTHERED WITH CRACKER CRUMBS AND SESAME SEEDS. "

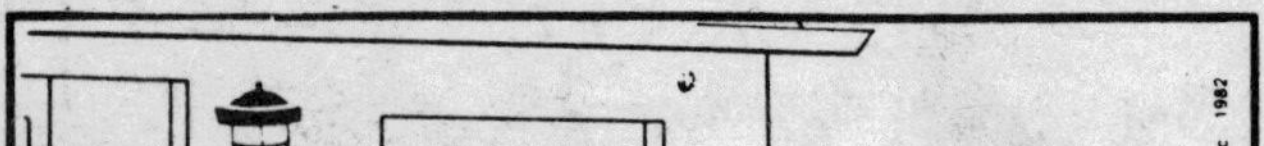

" WHEN I SAID 'GET THE PHONE,' I MEANT ANSWER IT. "

" HE ***WHAT*** ?? "

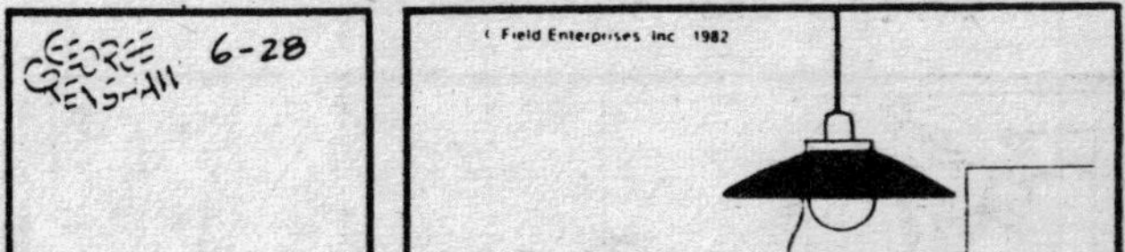

"ALL RIGHT, FINNEGAN, YOU SAY THIS FRISKY WHITE DOG BROKE INTO YOUR MAIL ROOM...

... AND WHAT HAPPENED?"

" INSTEAD OF THAT ALARM CLOCK, HAVE YOU CONSIDERED AN ELECTRIC CATTLE PROD ? "

" OH, GOOD. YOU'RE BATHING BELVEDERE. "

"YOUR CLEVER IMITATION OF JAMES CAGNEY...
LET'S SEE IT, NOW!"

" HE CALLS A SECRET NUMBER IN LAS VEGAS."

"I KNOW YOU'RE A LION-TAMER. THAT'S WHY I'VE COME TO YOU - NONE OF THE OBEDIENCE SCHOOLS WILL ACCEPT HIM."

" NO, NO. JUST ONE BALL AT A TIME ! "

"..MUST BE GETTING OLD.." " HE DOESN'T BOUNCE AS MUCH AS HE USED TO. "

"SINCE THIS IS YOUR FIRST FIGHT, I'M GONNA GO EASY ON YOU..."

"HE TRADED MY SPORTS CAR FOR *WHAT??*"

" I THINK HE WANTS STEAK AND RED WINE FOR DINNER TONIGHT."

" NOW, JUST ONE MINUTE! "

"WHY DID YOU EVER ASK HIM TO SLICE THE SALAMI?"

"TWO NECKS, THREE WINGS AND AN EXTRA BACK? I WISH I COULD HAVE SEEN **THAT** BIRD WHEN IT WAS ALIVE."

"YOUR FORM IS GOOD, BUT YOUR AIM IS A LITTLE OFF."

"FOR THE LAST TIME, I'M NOT MAKING YOU HOTCAKES FOR BREAKFAST."

"I RATE YOU A TEN, ORVY." "ON A SCALE OF ONE TO A HUNDRED!"

"ALL RIGHT, WHAT HAVE YOU BEEN UP TO **NOW**?"

"I JUST NOTICED - THESE ARE DOG VITAMIN PILLS I'VE BEEN TAKING ALL WEEK. DO YOU SUPPOSE THERE COULD BE SIDE EFFECTS?"

"OH, GOOD HEAVENS, IT'S ONLY A LITTLE DISTEMPER SHOT."

"YOU NEVER QUITE KNOW WHERE HE'LL TURN UP NEXT."

"I'M NEW ON THE ROUTE. NICE TO HAVE YOUR DOG NOT BARK AT ME."

"EVER NOTICE HOW POLITICIANS NEVER MAKE ANY PROMISES **AFTER** THEY'RE ELECTED?"

"WE NOW BRING YOU, DIRECT FROM WASHINGTON, 'TREASURY AGENTS GET THEIR MAN'."

"JUST EXACTLY WHAT DID YOU SAY IN YOUR NOTE WE SENT OFF IN THE BOTTLE?"

"NOT BAD CHOWDER. WHERE'D YOU GET THE FISH?"

"I HATE TO THINK HOW DISAPPOINTED HE'LL BE IF WE ***DON'T*** FIND ANY DINOSAUR EGGS."

"I HOPE I'M NOT BORING YOU."

"UM-BOY! I SNORE SO LOUD I WAKE MYSELF UP IN THE MIDDLE OF THE NIGHT." " TRY SLEEPING IN ANOTHER ROOM."

"DON'T WORRY... THEY'LL FIND US. I ADDRESSED THE NOTE TO OUR NEXT DOOR NEIGHBOR - THE ONE WHOSE YARD YOU TORE UP LAST MONTH."

"SPRING CLEANING."

"ARE YOU SURE WE'RE WATCHING A SOAP OPERA?"

"YOU CAN COME OUT NOW, DOCTOR BARKUM. THAT LAST DOG WASN'T BELVEDERE AFTER ALL."

"WHEN YOU HAVE HIS BADGE TAKEN AWAY, CAN I HAVE IT?"

"HAVE YOU NOTICED NEXT DOOR?...THE NEIGHBORS JUST GOT AN ADORABLE NEW FRENCH POODLE."

"NOW WHAT HAPPENED TO THAT FRESH SALAMI I JUST LAID OUT?"

"SHE GETS ABOUT 20 TO THE GALLON—PEDESTRIANS, THAT IS."

"GOOD TRY. BUT I DON'T THINK THE WORLD IS QUITE READY YET FOR BONE-FLAVORED ICE CREAM."

"WHY COULDN'T HE STICK TO JUST SNITCHING GARBAGE OUT OF PAILS?"

"HE JUST ATE THE WHOLE ROAST IN THE FRIDGE TO PROTEST THE UPPER VOLTA CRISIS, WHATEVER THAT IS."

"NOW THAT'S NOT GOING TO GET US SERVED ONE MINUTE SOONER."

" ACCORDING TO THIS A HOT DOG DELIVERY TRUCK WAS HIJACKED TODAY. "

" CAT ! "

"THERE'S GOT TO BE AN EASIER WAY TO PULL A TOOTH."

"WHAT A BEAUTIFUL DREAM. THERE WAS THIS BIG FOR SALE SIGN IN FRONT OF BELVEDERE'S HOUSE."

"A DRAG CHUTE? NOW THAT'S GOTTA BE ONE **FAST** POOCH."

"IT SAYS YOU'RE FAITHFUL, OBEDIENT, KIND, RESPECTFUL, REVERENT, CONSIDERATE AND LOYAL. IT HAS YOUR WEIGHT WRONG TOO."

" WHAT DID THE PLUMBER THINK OF YOUR SUGGESTION? "

" NOT IN MY OPINION. I SEE THE DODGERS FIRST, ASTROS SECOND, GIANTS... "

" WHIPLASH ! "

" WE'RE QUITE SATISFIED WITH OUR PRESENT DALMATIAN, THANK YOU. "

"SO YOU'RE VERY CLEVER AT MODELING WITH CLAY. BUT THAT WON'T SCARE OFF PEDDLERS AND YOU KNOW IT."

"AND I SAY YOU'RE SPOILING HIM."

"MAYDAY! MAYDAY!"

"NOW THAT I HAVE YOUR ATTENTION..." HOWZABOUT A NICE FRESH CRACKER?

"YOU'VE BEEN READING COMIC BOOKS AGAIN."

" WHY DID YOU HAVE TO ASK HIM TO HELP WITH THE SHRUB TRIMMING? "

" I CAN'T WAIT FOR YOUR NEW SURPRISE MILK SHAKE, OLD BUDDY. WHAT FLAVOR IS IT? "

" REMEMBER THE GOOD OLD DAYS WHEN HE USED TO JUST ROMP AROUND THE PARK? "

" NOVEMBER 3, 1843. NOTHING HAPPENED HERE."

" WHEN ARE WE GONNA GET A SOCIETY FOR THE PREVENTION OF CRUELTY TO HUMANS ? "

"I CAN'T UNDERSTAND IT. THIS BIRDCALL USED TO WORK REAL GOOD."

"ORVILLE NEVER DRINKS EXCEPT ON SPECIAL OCCASIONS.. TODAY STARTS NATIONAL CORN-FRITTER WEEK."

"LAY OFFA THAT WALKIE-TALKIE. THE POLICE, A FIRE CHIEF AND TWO PARAMEDICS ARE AT THE DOOR."

"I HOPE THAT ANSWERS YOUR QUESTION."

" THERE! *THAT* FENCE WILL KEEP BELVEDERE IN THE YARD FOR A WHILE!"

" WELL, HOW'S THE POPCORN COMING?"

"SO HE JUMPED INTO THE BACK OF YOUR TOOL TRUCK...MAYBE YOU SHOULDN'TA TALKED THAT WAY TO THE POOCH, CHARLIE."

" QUACK ! "

" MY STEAKS ARE ALMOST READY, OLD BUDDY. DID YOU SET THE TABLE ? "

" WOULDN'T IT BE BETTER IF WE JUST CALLED AN EXORCIST? "

" WARMING HIS BONES? "

" JUST GIVE US THE RUMOR, DEARIE.
DON'T CONFUSE US WITH FACTS. "

" NOW, WHAT IN HEAVEN'S NAME HAS HE BUILT ? "

"FEEL THAT UPDRAFT ?!"

"WELL, THERE'S ONE MORE DOG-CATCHER WE CAN FORGET ABOUT."

"HE'S JUST GIVING IT A DUMP TEST."

"THAT'S QUITE A HUNTING DOG YOU HAVE THERE, ORVILLE."

" VERY GOOD. NOW, LET'S TRY AGAIN FOR ACCURACY."

"SO WHO WAS GOING TO TIE WHOM OUT IN THE BACK YARD?"

"THEIR MARRIAGE HAS GIVEN NEW MEANING TO THE TERM 'MADLY IN LOVE'!"

" THIS IS NO TIME TO BE PLAYING GUESS WHO?! "

" IT'S ONE OF HIS EARLY ANCESTORS WHO BARKED AT THE FIRST WHEEL. "

" LET ME GIVE YOU A LITTLE TIP....YOU'RE STANDING TOO CLOSE TO THE BALL...AFTER YOU HIT IT. "

" YOU'RE LOOKING FIT AS A FIDDLE.... A BASS FIDDLE, THAT IS. "

"AND THE TROPHY FOR FINALLY CATCHING BELVEDERE WILL BE PRESENTED TO OFFICER HOOPER... WHEN HE GETS OUT OF THE HOSPITAL."

"WHY DON'T YOU JUST GO OVER AND INTRODUCE YOURSELF TO THE NEW POODLE NEXT DOOR?"

"SURE, HE LIKES TAKING HIS BATH. HE'S SITTING ON THE NEIGHBOR'S CAT."

"WHY CAN'T YOU JUST SWITCH OFF THE T.V. WHEN YOU DON'T LIKE THE PROGRAM ?"

"WHERE ARE YOUR 'SORRY OUR DOG RAIDED YOUR GARBAGE' CARDS ?"

"IT'S **NOT** CANNIBALISM! NOW CUT THAT OUT AND HAND ME AN EGG!"

" YOU'RE RIGHT. I THINK IT IS A RABBIT HOLE."

" BARKING AT PARKED CAR WHEELS ?... NOW IF THAT ISN'T THE HEIGHT OF LAZINESS! "

"THEY SPOIL THAT POOCH."

"I DON'T THINK HE'S LISTENING TO A WORD YOU'RE SAYING, FENTON."

"JUST SAY *HELP*. IT DOESN'T HAVE TO RHYME!"

"I'M MISSING A STRING OF WIENERS!"

"I THINK HE'S TRYING TO TELL US SOMETHING."

"VERY GOOD! VERY GOOD! YOU SHOULD GO A LONG WAY AS A BOOKKEEPER."

"CAN'T YOU DO ANYTHING RIGHT ?"

"I DON'T CARE IF IT IS NESTING SEASON!...
PUT 'EM BACK!"

"WELL, HERE-WE ARE - A WHOLE MILE OFFSHORE. WHAT A RELIEF TO GET OUT AND AWAY FROM 'OLD NOSY' FOR A SPELL."

" MOST FAMILY CRESTS HAVE EAGLES, LIONS AND SAINTS. YOURS HAS A GARBAGE CAN AND A FLEA BAG. "

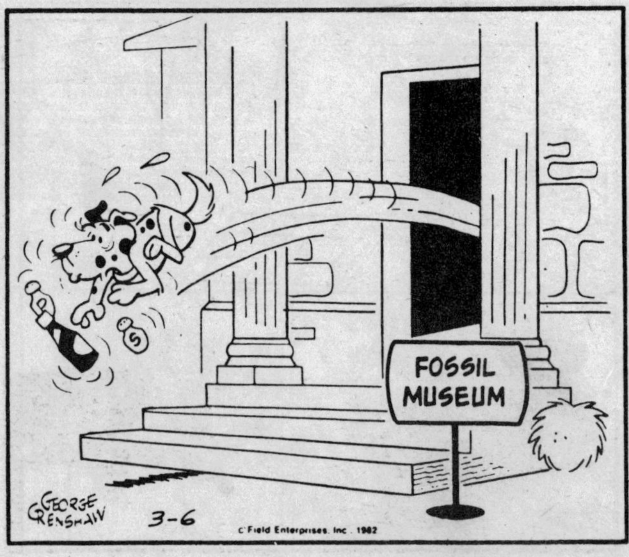

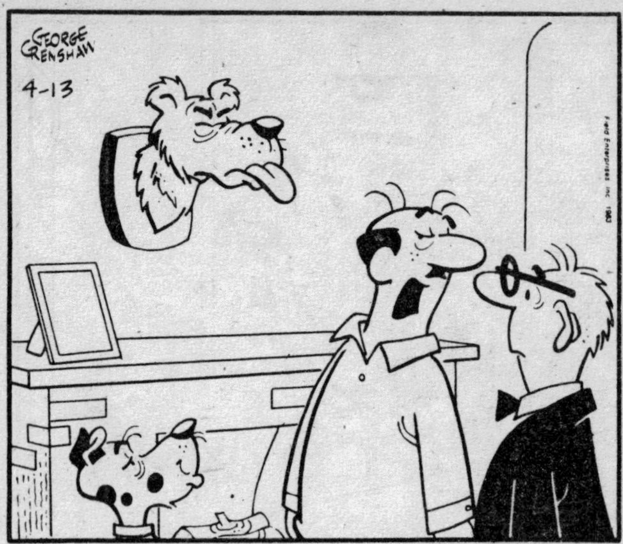

" DEFIANT RIGHT TO THE END. "

"EVER CONSIDER JUST BURYING THEM IN THE GROUND ?"

"JUST ***HOW*** EARLY ARE YOU TWO GOING FISHING?"

"I DON'T THINK HE HAS MUCH FAITH IN YOUR DRIVING ABILITY."

"TWO GRILLED CHEESE... FRENCH FRIES AND A SALAMI MALTED."

"HE DOESN'T BITE, BUT DON'T GET TOO CLOSE TO ORVILLE."

"YOU THREE ARE A PAIR IF THERE EVER WAS ONE."

"NO, YOU CANNOT USE THE CAR TONIGHT."

"THE MAILMAN BIT HIM."

"WHY DON'T YOU JUST TAKE OUT THE GARBAGE YOURSELF? YOU KNOW YOU ALWAYS LOSE!"

" OH, ALL RIGHT THEN. YOU CAN COME IN FOR THE NIGHT."

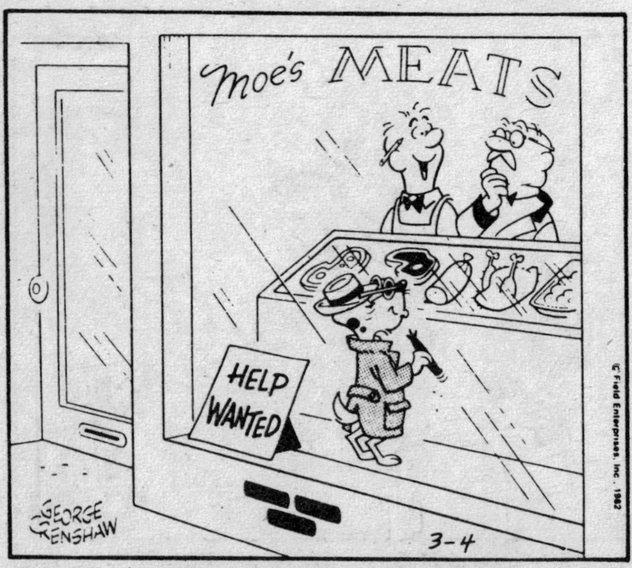

" HE SAYS HE'LL WORK FOR NOTHING, JUST TO LEARN THE BUSINESS."

" THAT'S WHAT I CALL A WATCHDOG. "

'NEXT TIME HE WAITS IN THE CAR!"

"AND HOW WERE THINGS AT LOCH NESS?"

" HE SELDOM GETS CAUGHT. "

"WHY CAN'T HE JUST CHASE CARS THE WAY OTHER DOGS DO?"

"GOOD NEWS, DEAR. BELVEDERE FIXED THE T.V. AND GOT RID OF THAT TERRIBLE HORIZONTAL STATIC."

"FORGET IT! IT'LL NEVER WORK!"

"NOW, ISN'T THAT SOMETHING? WE CAN'T GET HIM NEAR A DOGGIE BATH AT HOME!"

" LOOK... IF MY COOKING BOTHERS YOU THAT MUCH, JUST SAY SO. "

" ALL RIGHT- ISN'T IT ABOUT TIME YOU SWALLOWED YOUR PRIDE AND ADMITTED WE'RE LOST ? "

" I COULD HAVE SWORN I JUST BOUGHT A STRING OF WIENERS. "

" YOU PICKED A PRETTY DUMB PLACE TO AIR OUT A GREEN CARPET. "

" NO KIDDIN'... THE HEAD OFFICE SENT YOU TO REPLACE ME FOR THE REST OF THE WHOLE DAY ? "

"LOOK, IT'S EARLY IN THE MORNING. WHAT'S SO FUNNY?"

" NEVER SAY 'HIT ME' WHEN YOU PLAY BLACKJACK WITH BELVEDERE. "

" ALL RIGHT, ALL RIGHT, I'LL TAKE THE CEREAL THAT POPS. "

" HE SAYS HE'S SORRY HE WAS BAD AND WANTS TO COME BACK IN THE HOUSE. "

" HE WANTS TO KNOW WHICH LICENSE ? "

" SHE NOT ONLY TALKS TO HER PLANTS - WHEN SHE GOES ON A TRIP SHE SENDS THEM A POSTCARD. "

" ARE YOU TOGETHER ? "

" KNOCK IT OFF, OLD BUDDY, WE'RE IN ENOUGH TROUBLE WITHOUT THAT. "

" WHAT A NICE NEW SHOVEL. DID YOU GET A BOOK OF INSTRUCTIONS ? "

" WHY COULDN'T HE HAVE JUST GOTTEN INTERESTED IN A SIMPLE STAMP COLLECTION ? "

" ALL I KNOW IS, HE SAYS HE'S FROM THE TASTER'S OFFICE OF THE FOOD AND DRUG ADMINISTRATION. "

"I SUPPOSE THERE ARE CERTAIN DRAWBACKS TO HAVING A FEMALE BIRD AROUND THE HOUSE."

"I'M SORRY, WE DON'T TAKE TRADE-INS."

"WHY DON'T YOU GO OUT AND BREATHE IN THE CARBURETOR--
YOU MIGHT HELP THE CAR START."

"WHY COULDN'T YOU HAVE JUST BEEN SATISFIED WITH SOME OLD INDIAN ARROWHEADS OR A CLAY POT FOR A SOUVENIR?"

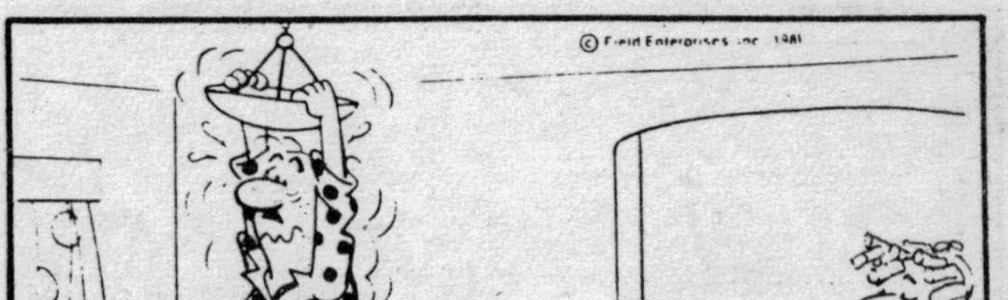

" DID YOU WAKE ORVILLE ? "

" IS THIS YOUR IDEA OF MY BIRTHDAY BREAKFAST IN BED ? "

"CAT."

"THAT'S NOT HOW WE EMPTY THE TRASH!"

"DON'T LET THAT NOISE SCARE YOU. BELVEDERE'S JUST WASHIN' HIS BONES."

"I DON'T THINK HE LIKES SLEEPING IN THE BASEMENT."

"I DON'T CARE IF IT IS YOUR MATING SEASON—
THE NEIGHBORS ARE COMPLAINING."

"YOU MUST BE HEARING THINGS. MY PHONE WASN'T RINGING."

" YOU CAN TAKE IT OFF NOW, OLD BUDDY. WE'RE PAST ALL THE GARBAGE PAILS."

"HE ALWAYS THINKS OF SOMETHING WHEN I RUN OUT OF AMMUNITION."

"NO, I DON'T HAVE THE ELECTRIC BLANKET. I THOUGHT YOU HAD IT."

" OH, NO... THE LAST TIME HE COOLED OFF LIKE THAT COST ME A $57 ICE CREAM BILL."

"WHY DON'T YOU JUST TAKE THE PENALTY STROKE?"

" DON'T LET ME DISTURB YA, FELLAS. I JUST CAME DOWN TO CHECK ON MY ALLIGATOR."

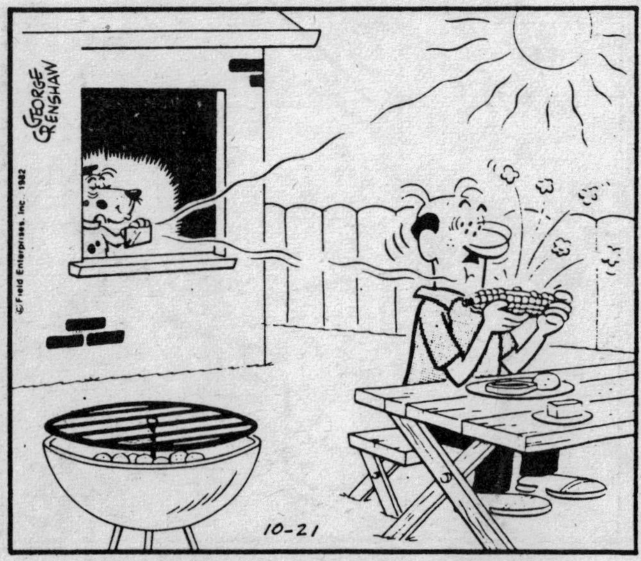

"LOOK...THERE ARE **THREE** OF US GOING ON THIS TRIP."

" SURE, I PAID BELVEDERE A DOLLAR TO WASH THE CAR. WHAT'S THE PROBLEM ? "

" SHOW BELVEDERE IN NOW. "

" IT'S THE SAME POOCH AGAIN - WITH A DIFFERENT POODLE EVERY DAY. HE'S OUR BEST CUSTOMER. "

" ALL AT ONCE, ORVILLE'S INTELLIGENCE ISN'T BEING INSULTED, I SEE. "

"OF COURSE THEY'RE NICE AND TENDER. BELVEDERE PRE-CHEWS ALL THE HARD ONES."

"HE'S GETTING WARM, EH, ORV?"

"BOY! THAT WAS SOME WHIRLPOOL!"

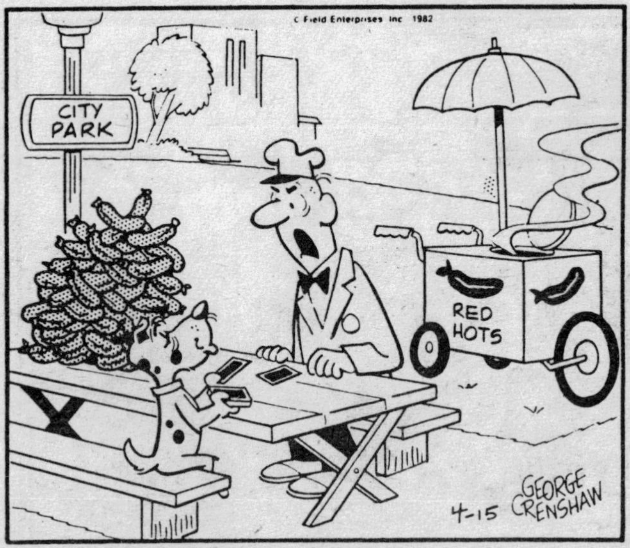

" SHUT UP AND DEAL! "

"DID YOU WIPE THE MUD FROM YOUR FEET LIKE I TOLD YOU?"

" ALL RIGHT. WHO'S BEEN AT MY WATER CANTEEN ? "

"OH, HE'S FINE, MRS. DIBBLE. I'M JUST SITTING HERE READING HIM A STORY."

"CITY DOG POUND...WHAT'S THAT, SIR?"

"WELL, WHATTAYA KNOW! IT'S STARTING TO WARM UP ALL OF A SUDDEN!"

"WE COULD ONLY AFFORD ONE HAMMOCK THIS YEAR."

" IT WAS A CASE OF DOUBLE PARKING. WE WERE ON TOP OF ANOTHER CAR. "

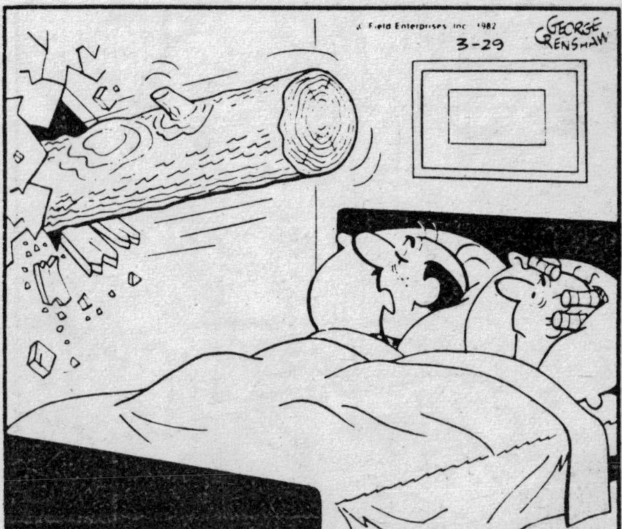

" I THINK HE WANTS IN. "

" I DIDN'T **THINK** THAT SOUNDED LIKE ORVILLE'S USUAL MORNING MUMBLE. "

" BUT HE'S BUYING ! "

" LOOK, IF YOU WANTED IN, WHY DIDN'T YOU JUST RING THE BELL ? "

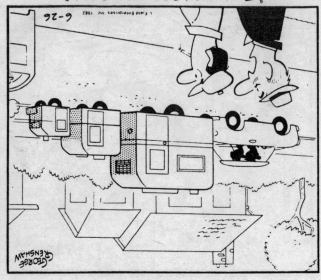

" THEY HAVE A DOG AND A BIRD. "

"YOU FINISHED PUTTING IN THE EXTENSION?... WHAT EXTENSION?"

"I'VE NEVER SEEN HIM BEFORE EITHER."

" WHATAYA MEAN THE CAR'S FLOODED ? "

" HE'S GOING ALL OUT TO MAKE AN IMPRESSION ON THAT CUTE CHIHUAHUA NEXT DOOR.

"NOW THERE'S A DOGGIE TRICK YOU SELDOM SEE!"

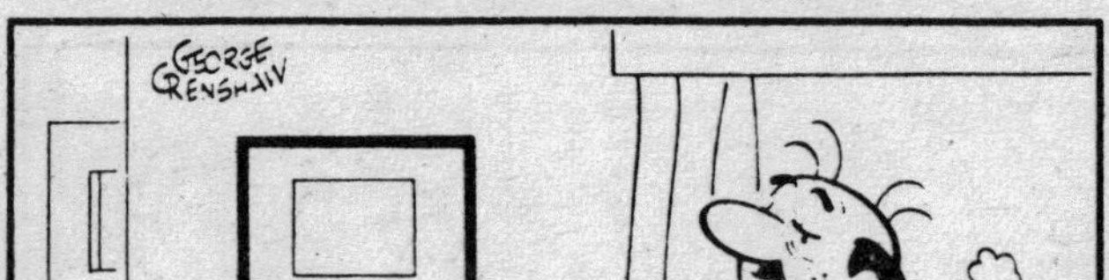

"OF COURSE I'M GLAD YOU WON BEST OF BREED. AND NO, I WILL NOT ADDRESS YOU IN THE FUTURE AS 'YOUR GRACE.'"

" I THINK HE KNOWS WE'RE IN SKUNK COUNTRY. "

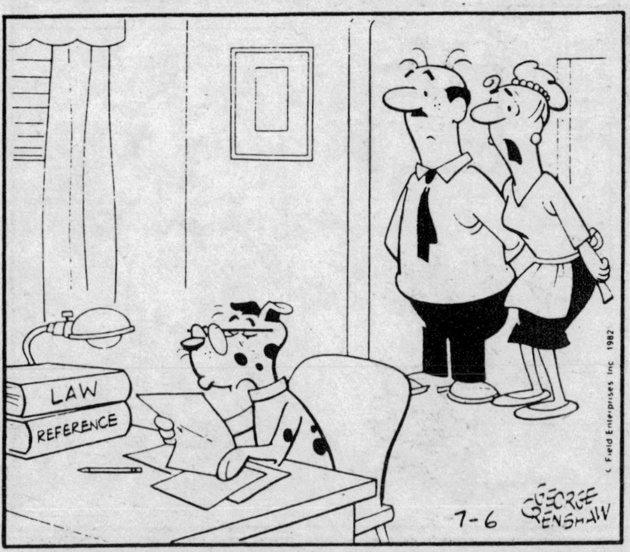

" I SNEAKED EXTENDER INTO HIS HAMBURGER.
I THINK HE'S PLANNING TO SUE US. "

"THAT'S THE LAST TIME I'M LETTING YOU DO THE PACKING."

"A THOUSAND GARBAGE CANS IN TOWN AND YOU HAD TO PICK THE ALLEY BACK OF FRANKENBLITZ CASTLE!"

" ADMIT IT! YOU'VE BEEN PLAYING STRIP POKER AGAIN, HAVEN'T YOU? "

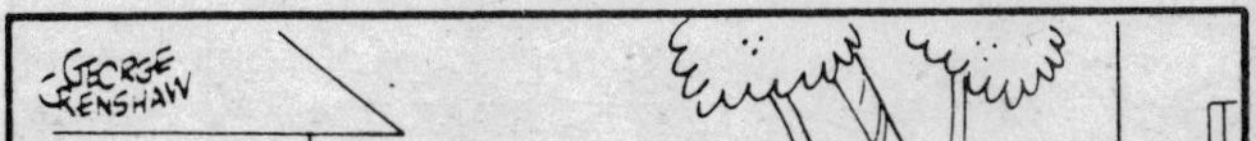

" HE SAID OUR GARBAGE WAS QUITE GOOD TODAY AND GAVE ME A TIP. "

" THERE NOW. NEXT TIME I HOPE YOU'LL KNOW BETTER THAN TO CHASE A PARKED CAR. "

" THERE'S NOTHING LIKE LOOKING AT VACATION PICTURES TO PUT GUESTS IN A TRAVELING MOOD. "

"WHAT DO YOU KNOW ABOUT THIS BILL FROM THE ABC LANGUAGE SCHOOL FOR FRENCH LESSONS?"

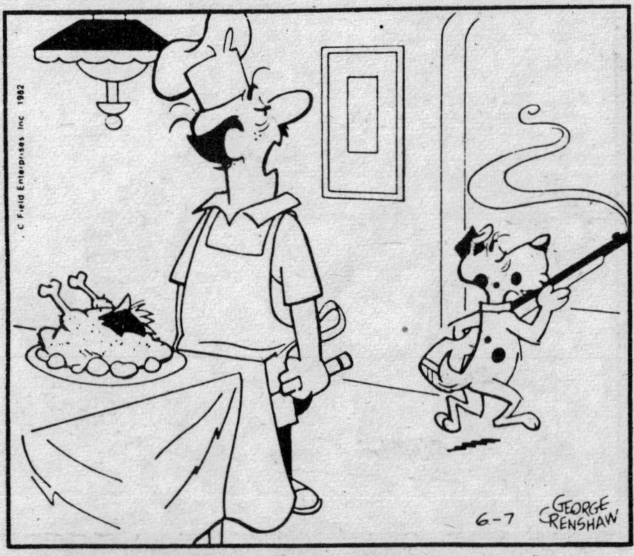

"IT WASN'T **THAT** UNDER-COOKED!"

I'LL ADMIT HE'S A LAZY WATCHDOG, BUT WE'RE SURE NOT BOTHERED WITH PROWLERS!"

"GOOD HEAVENS, ONE HAM SANDWICH WON'T SPOIL HIS APPETITE FOR DINNER."

"NO MATTER WHAT, HE ALWAYS GOES FIRST CLASS."

"HE EMPHATICALLY DENIES RAIDING OUR GARBAGE AND SAYS IT TASTED LOUSY ANYWAY."

"SOME WEIRD VOICE FROM THE HEAD OFFICE...THEY'RE SENDING OVER A NEW MAN TO HELP WITH THE HAMBURGER AND WIENERS."

" NOW YOU SHOULD HAVE ASKED MR. PERKINS FIRST. MAYBE HE DIDN'T WANT TO PLAY 'BOPPO'. "

"JUST WHERE DID YOU GET THESE EGGS?"

" THIS IS THE LIMIT! WE CAN NEVER GET HIM TO EAT LIVER AT HOME ! "

"HAVEN'T YOU WHEEDLED ENOUGH BONES FOR ONE DAY?"

"A VERY CATCHY TUNE! NOW, WITH NEW WORDS AND DIFFERENT MUSIC, I THINK YOU'LL HAVE A HIT."

"ER...YES, IT'S LAST YEAR'S LICENSE...BUT WE'RE ONLY SHOOTING AT THE ONES WE MISSED LAST YEAR."

" WE FORGOT THE CALL WHISTLE. "

"I GIVE UP. WHAT HAS TWO HEADS, IS 60 FEET LONG AND SWIMS?"

"WITH MEAT PRICES WHAT THEY ARE, MAYBE HE'S JUST PAYING YOU A COMPLIMENT WHEN HE CALLS YOU **MEATHEAD**."

"WELL, SO LONG, RONNIE.... GIVE MY REGARDS TO NANCY."

" ALL I KNOW IS HE CHASES A LOT OF CARS AND WANTS A QUART OF JET FUEL. "

" JUST WALK THE LINE, FELLA, JUST WALK THE LINE."

" A BONE-OF-THE-MONTH CLUB ? "

"GOOD GRIEF, IF HE WANTED TO COOK SOMETHING, WHY DID YOU LET HIM READ YOUR BRANDY FRICASSEE RECIPE ? "

"EXCELLENT! IT'S BEEN YEARS SINCE I'VE EATEN A ZEBRA."

"I CAN TOLERATE COMEDIES WITH A LAUGH TRACK...BUT ANTACID COMMERCIALS WITH A GURGLE TRACK?"

"OH, DON'T ACT SO PUT OUT. HE JUST WANTS TO CHECK THE DOG FOOD ADS."

"I DON'T CARE **HOW** I CAME HOME LAST NIGHT. DIG THAT WALKWAY **STRAIGHT** LIKE IT'S SUPPOSED TO BE!"

"IT SEEMS TO BE WORKING. HE THINKS WE'RE ONE OF THEM."

"WHAT DO YOU MEAN, 'WUPPS, TOO BAD'? I HAVEN'T EVEN STARTED YET."

" HE INVENTED A **WHAT** ? "

"ALL RIGHT. LET'S SEE THIS NEW INVENTION FOR GETTING ORVILLE UP IN THE MORNINGS."

" WE SHOULD HAVE WARNED YOU... NEVER MENTION **CAT GUT** IN FRONT OF JEZEBEL. "

" SO YOU WENT HUNTING AND FOUND A GIANT CONDOR EGG. SO WHAT ? "

" YOU GAVE EIGHT FILET STEAKS TO THE DELIVERY BOY? WE DON'T HAVE A DELIVERY BOY ! "

" IT'S CERTAINLY A PLEASURE NOT HAVING THAT NOISY POOCH AROUND TODAY."

" IT'S HIS BIRTHDAY, SO I GIFT-WRAPPED IT. "

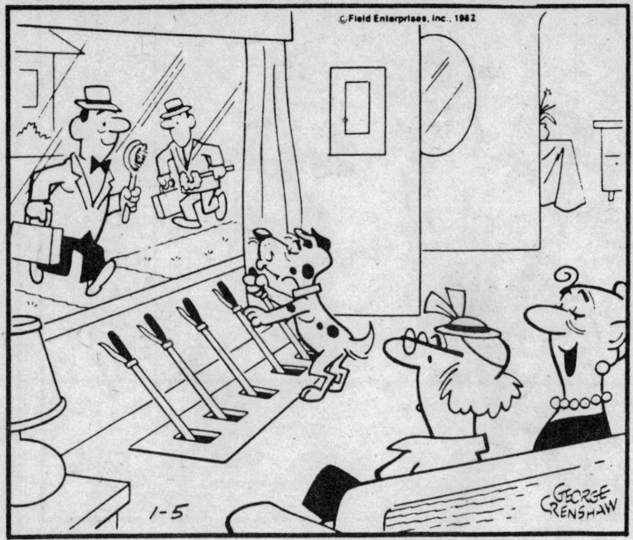

" BELVEDERE HAS HIS OWN SPECIAL WAY OF DEALING WITH PEDDLERS. "

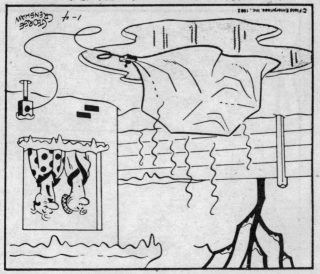

"YOU WERE WONDERING WHAT HAPPENED TO YOUR ELECTRIC BLANKET ?"

" DIS IS A STICK-UP ! "

" HE'S SO SERIOUS ABOUT LOSING WEIGHT - HE'S ON FIVE DIFFERENT DIETS AT ONCE. "

" SEND ONE TO THE STOCK MARKET. "

" I THINK HE'S MASTERMINDED AN ALL-OUT NEIGHBORHOOD GARBAGE CAN RAID. "

"LOOK, WHEN I ASKED YOU TO HELP WITH THE CLEANING, I DIDN'T MEAN CLEANING OUT THE REFRIGERATOR."

"DID YOU HEAR A PEEP?"

"DON'T WORRY ABOUT CHI CHI, DEAR. SHE ALWAYS WAITS RIGHT THERE WHILE I SHOP."

"I TOLD YOU THAT PADLOCK WOULDN'T KEEP HIM OUT."

"HOW COME EVERY TIME YOU GO ON A SEVEN-DAY DIET, YOU ALWAYS FINISH IT IN TWO DAYS?"

"THIS SHOULD PROVE INTERESTING."

" YOU KNOW, YOU COULD TAKE A PENALTY STROKE AND JUST MOVE THE BALL. "

" YOU WERE SNORING TOO LOUD AGAIN. "

"IF GOD HAD WANTED YOU TO PLAY THE PIANO, HE'D HAVE GIVEN YOU 88 FINGERS."

"I UNDERSTAND THERE'S A BIG WATER HAZARD ON THIS HOLE."

" ALL I KNOW IS, HE CAN OUTJUMP EVERY KID IN THE NEIGHBORHOOD. "

" HE'S REVIEWING HIS FIGHT FILMS ?"

"SURE IT'S LOADED WITH PRESERVATIVES, BUT AT YOUR AGE YOU NEED ALL THE PRESERVATIVES YOU CAN GET."

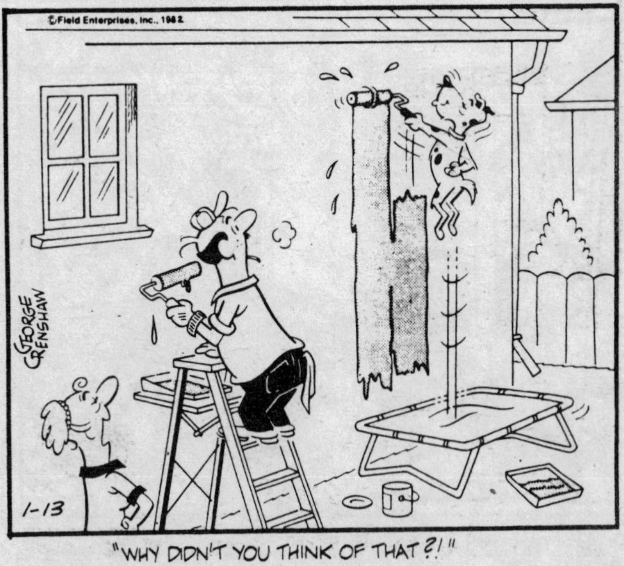

"WHY DIDN'T YOU THINK OF THAT?!"

" AND NOW, AN IMPORTANT MESSAGE FROM YOUR SPONSOR: **GO OUTSIDE AND ROMP!** "

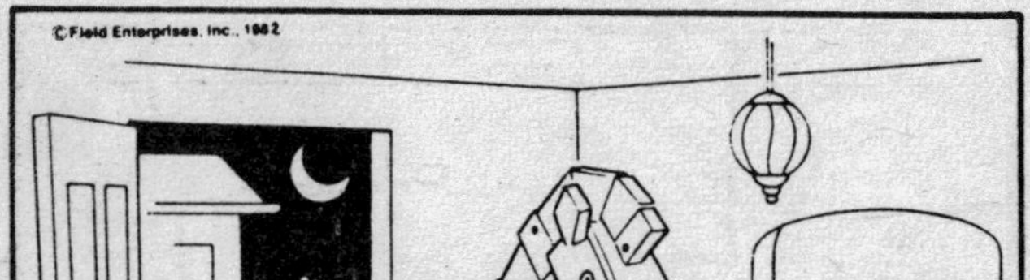

" HE'LL GO TO ANY LENGTH JUST TO GET IN FOR THE NIGHT! "

" GUESS WHAT ? I LEARNED A NEW WORD TODAY. "

" WE GAVE UP YEARS AGO TRYING TO CONVINCE HIM HE WAS A DOG. "

" WE DON'T LIKE MOBILES ! "

" ALL RIGHT! WHAT HAPPENED TO MY PITCHER OF BEER I LEFT HERE ? "

"WELL, OLD BUDDY, WHAT OTHER SECRET FISHING SPOTS DO YOU KNOW OF THAT NOT EVEN THE BEARS HAVE HEARD OF?"

"HE SHOULD WIN THE TALENT."

"THAT'S WHAT I DON'T LIKE ABOUT THIS COUNTRY... THESE SUDDEN GUSTS OF WIND OUT OF NOWHERE."

"I THINK MAYBE HE'S SERIOUS ABOUT RUNNING AWAY THIS TIME!"

"NOW WHAT IN BLAZES HAPPENED TO MY FALSE TEETH?"

"ALL RIGHT-YOU WANTED ME TO TEACH YOU TO BOX. LET'S GO!"

" HOLD THE FRENCH FRIES ! "

"WITH EVERYONE COMING, I'M AFRAID THE TURKEY ISN'T LARGE ENOUGH. WHAT'LL WE DO?"

"ALL I KNOW IS THEY HAVE A CAT AND THEY SPOIL HER A LOT."

" IT'S ALL RIGHT. I TOLD HIM HE COULD HAVE ***ONE*** PIECE OF CAKE."

"I WARNED YOU NOT TO SEND HIM OUT TO GET MILK!"

"WHY CAN'T JEZEBEL JUST CATERWAUL AT NIGHT LIKE OTHER FELINES DO?"

"ALL RIGHT, SUPPOSE SOME INSECT DID GET INTO MY VITAMINS DURING THE NIGHT. SO WHAT?"

"ALL RIGHT, WHO ATE ALL MY MULTI-VITAMIN PILLS?"

" SUN'S UP, OLD BUDDY. LET'S SEE WHAT OUR TRAPS CAUGHT TODAY . "

" I THINK WE'RE IN FOR A COLD **COLD** WINTER. "

"DOES HE ALWAYS HAVE TO MAKE A BIG THING OF IT, EVERY TIME I COME OUT THE DRIVEWAY?"

"YOU CALL THAT A BANANA SPLIT?"

" HE ADDS FOOD-EXTENDER WHEN THE PAILS ARE ONLY HALF FULL. "

" YOU FORGOT TO SAY GOODBYE TO HIM. "

"LOOK, OLD BUDDY-OUR CAMPING TRIP ENDED YESTERDAY."

" WELL, THAT'S ONE MORE BRAND OF DOG FOOD HE DOESN'T LIKE. "

" MOST DOGS HATE A BATH. "

" I THINK WE MAY HAVE FINALLY PUT A STOP TO HIS GARBAGE-PAIL RAIDING. "

" WELL, SO MUCH FOR TRIPLE-LOCKING THE DOOR TO KEEP HIM OUT."

" FIRST WE TAUGHT HIM TO BRING IN THE PAPER, AND NOW HE HAS HIS OWN PAPER ROUTE. "

"JUST WHAT KIND OF A COCKTAIL DID YOU FIX FOR ORVILLE?"

"I DON'T LIKE THAT FAST BUNCH HE'S RUNNING AROUND WITH!"

"I THINK HE WANTS IN!"

"... OF COURSE I'LL ACCEPT THE CHARGES!"

"NOW! LET'S TRY IT ONCE AGAIN."

"SINCE YOU STOPPED DIGGING UP THE YARD, JUST WHERE HAVE YOU BEEN STASHING YOUR OLD BONES?"

"YOU CAN ALWAYS SPOT AN OLD RETIRED PUPPETEER."

"WHAT'S THIS BILL FROM FLOOGLE'S FISH MARKET FOR 200 POUNDS OF FRESH SALMON ?"

"THERE'S SOMEONE HERE TO SEE THE HEAD OF THE HOUSE."

"VERY CLEVER INVENTION, BUT I DON'T NEED TRAINING WHEELS TO WEAR DURING MY HAPPY HOUR."

" I TOLD YOU NOT TO PRACTICE YOUR POLE VAULTING SO CLOSE TO THE HOUSE. "

" WHY DID YOU EVER EVEN LOAN HIM THE CAR KEYS IN THE FIRST PLACE ? "

"I HOPE THERE'S A HAPPY ENDING TO THIS MOVIE, LIKE MAYBE THE HERO SHOOTING THE AUTHOR."

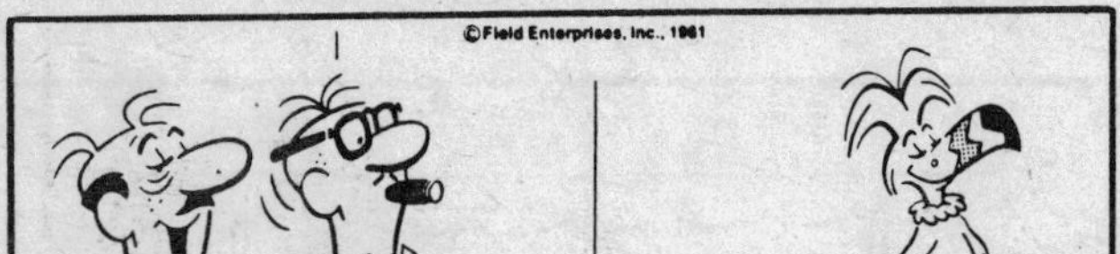

"NOW THAT YOU MENTION IT, YES, CHI CHI IS A TALKING BIRD."

"OH, COME NOW. WE'RE ONLY GOING TO THE VET'S FOR YOUR DISTEMPER SHOT. YOU DON'T HAVE TO MAKE OUT YOUR LAST WILL AND TESTAMENT."

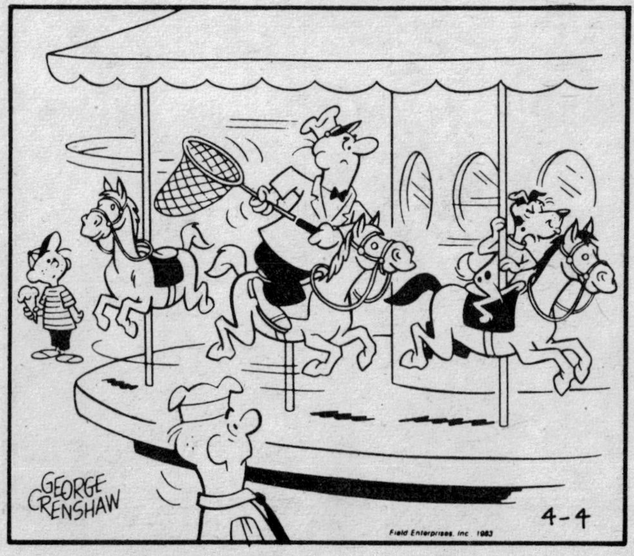

"IT'S GOOD, BUT WHO'D BUY A BOOK ON *HOW TO TRAIN PEOPLE* ?"

"ANY OTHER COLLATERAL ?"

"NOW ISN'T THAT A NICE HUNTING DOG? HE'S EVEN CLEANING YOUR GUN!"

"IT WAS CUTE AT FIRST. NOW SHE HAS THE HABIT."

" RELAX! IF YOU'VE SEEN ONE DESERT RAT YOU'VE SEEN 'EM ALL! "

" NOW STOP THAT, AND HAND ME BACK MY VIOLIN! "

"YOU DON'T SEE MANY DOG HOUSES THESE DAYS WITH A BOWLING ALLEY."

"OUR CAT JEZEBEL IS THE BEST MOUSER ON THE BLOCK."

"ALL I KNOW IS WHAT I READ IN THE PAPERS."

"ALL I KNOW IS WHAT I READ ON BUMPER STICKERS."

"PERHAPS YOU NEVER SHOULD HAVE MENTIONED MR. TUTTLE WORKS AT THE PACKING HOUSE, DEAR."

"I JUST TOLD HIM HE'S NOT IN THE GUINNESS BOOK OF RECORDS FOR THE MOST GARBAGE PAILS RAIDED."

"I UNDERSTAND BELVEDERE AND OUR NEW NEIGHBOR HAD QUITE A FALLING-OUT LAST NIGHT."

" SURE, WE'RE PLAYING FOR A DOLLAR A HOLE. BUT DON'T LET HIS OVERCONFIDENCE SHAKE YOU UP. "

" WHEN YOU LET HIM TAKE UP SCULPTURE, I THOUGHT HE'D BE A LITTLE MORE CREATIVE. "

" I THINK HE MEANS TO RUN AWAY **FOR GOOD** THIS TIME. "

"JUST WHAT ARE YOU TRYING TO SUGGEST ABOUT MY BOOKKEEPING ? "

"DID YOU HAVE TO ORDER IN FRENCH?"

"YOU SHOT AN 88? GREAT...THAT'S GREAT! THEN, WHAT DID YOU SHOOT ON THE SECOND NINE HOLES?"

"OH, ALL RIGHT. I'LL FIX THE LEAK IN YOUR DOGHOUSE."

"I NEED A NINE-LETTER WORD FOR 'GLUTTON.' I TRIED 'BELVEDERE', BUT IT DIDN'T WORK."

"CUT THAT OUT!"

"WOULD YOU BELIEVE...THERE'S A TUNNEL IN THERE THAT LEADS ALL THE WAY TO THE NEIGHBOR'S WINE CELLAR."

"LOOPHOLES, KICKBACKS, FLIMFLAM, SKULDUGGERY, WHEEDLING AND DOUBLE-SHUFFLE. HOW'S THAT FOR A LITTLE QUIBBLE TO SPARK YOUR GUILE?"

" THEY'RE BLACKTOPPING OUR STREET TODAY. I JUST HOPE BELVEDERE DOESN'T BOTHER THE MEN TOO MUCH."

"WHEN HE SAID HE WAS GOING TO BAKE CHOCOLATE CHIP COOKIES, I THOUGHT HE MEANT FOR EVERYONE."

"GET READY. I THINK IT'S WORKING!"

" PREHISTORIC SOCIETY? FOSSIL DEPARTMENT? WHY SHOULD THEY BE CALLING US? "

" SAY, ORVIE, ARE YOU AN INTROVERT OR AN EXTROVERT OR JUST A PLAIN, ORDINARY EVERYDAY VERT? "

"LET'S GO, PIEDGRASS—WE'LL GET THE BEST OF **HIM** TODAY."

"DID YOU HAVE TO TELL CHI CHI THE BIRD-WATCHERS WERE IN TOWN?"

" I FOUND YOUR COLORING FOR THE EASTER EGGS."

" I KNOW HE'S BEEN A NAUGHTY DOGGIE, BUT DON'T YOU THINK YOUR PUNISHMENT IS A BIT SEVERE ? "

BELVEDERE

by

by GEORGE CRENSHAW

TOR

A TOM DOHERTY ASSOCIATES BOOK